Who Is
Steven Spielberg?

Who Is
Steven Spielberg?

By Stephanie Spinner
Illustrated by Daniel Mather

Grosset & Dunlap
An Imprint of Penguin Group (USA) LLC

For Jane O'Connor, friend extraordinaire—SS

For Katie and The Wombat—DM

GROSSET & DUNLAP
Published by the Penguin Group
Penguin Group (USA) LLC, 375 Hudson Street, New York, New York 10014, USA

USA | Canada | UK | Ireland | Australia | New Zealand | India | South Africa | China

penguin.com
A Penguin Random House Company

Library of Congress Control Number: 2013032702

ISBN 978-0-448-47935-4   10 9 8 7 6 5

Contents

Who Is
Steven Spielberg?

When Steven Spielberg was ten, he borrowed
his father's movie camera. He used it to film all
kinds of things—model-train wrecks, camping
trips, and even the hubcaps on the family car. In
fact, he borrowed the camera so often that his
father finally gave it to him. From that day on,
the Spielberg living room became a movie set,
cluttered with props.

    While other kids played sports, Steven dreamed up stories to film. Instead of doing homework, he wrote scripts. He figured out how to use lighting, sound, and camera angles to get the effects he wanted. He developed the knack of persuading his parents, his sisters, and anybody else who was around to put on costumes and act for him. Luckily for Steven, his parents encouraged him, and so did his friends. The very first time he showed one of his short movies to the members of his Boy Scout troop, they shouted and cheered.

Their applause only confirmed what Steven already knew: that his favorite place in the world was behind a camera.

Today, just about everybody knows who Steven Spielberg is. He directed four of the most successful films of all time: *Jaws, Indiana Jones and the Raiders of the Lost Ark, E.T.: The Extra-Terrestrial*, and *Jurassic Park*. He's won two Oscars for Best Director and an Oscar for Best Picture. He's produced dozens of films and

television shows, created video games, and headed up his own movie studio. His work has dazzled fans all over the world.

But his favorite place is still behind a movie camera. Chances are, it always will be.

Chapter 1
Brownie Hog

Steven Allan Spielberg was born on December 18, 1946, in Cincinnati, Ohio. World War II was finally over, and the country was getting back to normal. In the mid-forties that meant fathers commuted to their jobs, most mothers stayed home with their kids, cars were American, and telephones were connected to wires. It was a time when middle-class families flocked to the suburbs. Life there was safe, peaceful, and just a little bit dull.

Steven grew up in suburbia, but his household was far from dull. His parents, Leah Posner and Arnold Spielberg, were Jewish, the children of immigrants. Though they were both from Cincinnati, they didn't meet until 1942, after

Arnold had enlisted in the army. Shortly after
their first and only date, he was shipped off to
fight in Burma, a small Asian country on the
other side of the world. But he and Leah wrote to
each other until he came home in 1944, and they
were married the next year.

Arnold loved science and machines. After
finishing his studies in electrical engineering,
he quickly found work in the brand-new field of
computer science. At that time computers were the

size of entire rooms, and few people knew about them. Arnold was one of the first.

Leah came from a devout family that was also very creative. She had relatives in vaudeville and the theater. One of her uncles was a lion tamer— a fairly unusual profession for someone in an Orthodox Jewish family.

It was difficult to find a place where the family could put down roots. Because Arnold was such an outstanding engineer, he was always being offered new and better jobs—which meant that the Spielbergs moved a lot.

They went from Ohio, where Steven was born, to Camden, New Jersey. After his sister Anne was born, the family moved to Haddon Township, New Jersey, where his sisters Sue and Nancy were born. When Nancy was still a baby, they moved to Phoenix, Arizona.

Going from one school to another was hard for Steven. As soon as he got to know kids his own age, the family was on the move again. He was

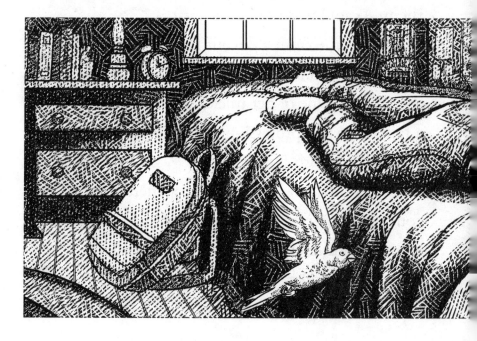

always the new boy in class and spent a lot of his childhood feeling like an outsider. In Phoenix his refuge was his cluttered bedroom. He kept turtles, free-flying parakeets, and a lizard in there, and he wrote stories instead of doing his homework. Steven often longed for a friend who was as different as he was. Sometimes he thought that a small, kindly alien would be ideal.

Years later, Steven made *E.T.: The Extra-Terrestrial*, one of the most popular movies of all time. But in 1957, kids like Steven didn't make movies; they watched them. That changed on Father's Day, when Leah gave Arnold a movie camera.

It was an eight-millimeter Brownie—inexpensive and easy to operate—the kind people used for home movies. Steven couldn't wait to borrow it. At first he staged and filmed crashes

with his Lionel trains and watched the films
over and over. He thought they were great. His
dad's movies, on the other hand, were blurry
and boring. Steven had lots of suggestions for
improving them, but his father had a better idea.
He simply gave Steven the camera.

Steven took on the job of filming the family's camping trips. He got his parents and sisters to wear costumes, gave them parts to play, and told them how and where to move. As young as he was, he quickly mastered the Brownie and began taking it with him everywhere.

In the Boy Scouts he made a nine-minute Western to earn a merit badge in photography. He cast his fellow Scouts as cowboys, and when he screened it for them, the troop went wild—shouting, whistling, and cheering. "In that moment," Steven said later, "I knew what I wanted to do with the rest of my life." He was eleven years old.

Chapter 2
Nerdy but Cool

Steven was used to being called a nerd. He didn't play baseball or football, and he could barely run a mile. He was practically invisible to girls. He was short and skinny. He stammered, he bit his nails, and he was Jewish. In Phoenix, a city

with very few Jewish families, that made him a little different.

But with a camera, he was less lonely and less of an outsider. He made one short film after another. First came *Fighter Squad*, about World War II pilots in action. After filming the cockpit of a plane at a local airport, he combined his footage with old newsreels showing actual US fighter planes in the air. It looked pretty convincing, especially to his friends.

In 1962 he completed *Escape to Nowhere*, about US soldiers trying to escape enemy troops in the African desert. The Arizona desert near Steven's neighborhood made a great substitute for the real thing.

Most ambitious of all was *Firelight*, a two-hour science-fiction movie about alien kidnappings. It took Steven a year to finish and cost $800. That was a truly big budget for a kid back then, but Steven took it in stride. Now sixteen, he was learning how to make action pictures with no driver's license, very little money, and parents who wouldn't let him go out unless he did his homework.

Luckily, his parents were almost always encouraging. Arnold got Steven permission to film the airport and the plane for *Fighter Squad*. Leah made the soldiers' costumes for *Escape to Nowhere* and drove the family's old army jeep into the desert so Steven could film it.

Arnold donated $500 to *Firelight*'s budget, and when it was finished, he rented a theater in Phoenix for the opening. Standing on a tall, shaky ladder, Leah put the film's title up on the marquee. She had already invited the whole neighborhood to make sure that the theater was full. On the evening of March 24, 1964, the family rode to the theater in

a limousine. Steven had paid for it so they could arrive in style. It was a happy occasion for all of them.

While Steven was making his early movies, his social life improved a lot. He found out that giving his classmates acting parts was like inviting them to a really great party. And they all wanted to come.

Steven was sixteen when *Escape to Nowhere* won first prize in an amateur-film contest, the Canyon Films Junior Film Festival. Exciting as that was, it couldn't make up for the fact that the Spielbergs were moving again. This time it was to Saratoga, California, where his dad would be working for IBM, the computer company.

For Steven, far worse than the move was the news that his parents were separating. The family broke apart slowly and painfully in California. After filing for divorce, Leah moved back to Arizona with Anne, Sue, and Nancy. Steven stayed with Arnold in California. It was the unhappiest time in his life. Yet the move brought him much closer to the center of the film industry—which was exactly where he belonged.

Chapter 3
Studio Stowaway

Saratoga, California, less than fifty miles from San Francisco, is now part of Silicon Valley. But in 1964 it was just another small, middle-class suburb. Saratoga High, Steven's new school, wasn't all that different from Arcadia High in Phoenix.

Unlike many teenagers in the mid-1960s, he wasn't interested in drugs, rock and roll, or politics. All he cared about was breaking into the movie business, any way he could.

His chance came the summer before his senior year of high school. While visiting cousins in Los Angeles, Steven took a tour of Universal Studios. He

was soon fidgeting with boredom. He had zero interest in seeing things like the street set of *Leave It to Beaver*, a 1950s television show. He wanted to go behind the scenes, to view the studio's inner workings. So he left the tour during a bathroom break and wandered around the vast lot by himself, trying to look as if he belonged.

That worked until a man named Chuck Silvers spotted him. Silvers, Universal's film librarian, guessed correctly that this skinny, long-haired kid in jeans was not a studio employee. But after a few minutes of conversation, he was so impressed with Steven that he gave him a three-day pass to the lot.

It was Steven's ticket to heaven. The next day, wearing his ill-fitting bar-mitzvah suit and a tie, and carrying a briefcase with a candy bar in it, he strolled past the guard at the gate. He did it again for the next two days, and each time the guard, called Scotty, waved him in. Steven never had to show his pass.

Delighted with the laid-back security system, Steven kept coming to the studio every day for weeks, always in his rumpled suit. He roamed around the sound stages, taking notes. One day he found an empty office on the lot, so he called the switchboard and had the office's phone hooked up. Then, with the office as a base, he spent his days hanging around sets; talking with directors, editors, and actors; and learning everything he could about the business. It was the education of his dreams. Even getting kicked off an Alfred Hitchcock set was a thrill.

Returning to high school for his senior year
was quite a letdown. So was getting rejected by
the film schools at the University of Southern
California and the University of California, Los
Angeles, because of his poor grades. The only
school that would take him was California State
College at Long Beach, and it didn't even have
a film department. Steven didn't want to go,
but his parents felt differently. And though he

wasn't getting along with either of them, they did help him face reality: It was 1965, the country was at war again, and if he didn't go to college, he would be drafted into the army and sent to fight in Vietnam. Even a college without a film department was better than taking part in a war he didn't believe in.

So Steven enrolled at Long Beach as an English major, went to as few classes as possible, and spent most of his time at Universal Studios.

To actually get a paying job at a studio like Universal, Steven had to persuade people to take a look at his films. And that was a lot harder than getting past Scotty at the security gate. All Steven's movies were on eight-millimeter film, because it was the cheapest to buy and process. Professionals worked in thirty-five-millimeter, which provided better images but was much more expensive. Anything else was considered kid stuff—not worth watching.

The situation was frustrating, but now Steven's luck, which had been good so far, got even better. A young producer agreed to pay for Steven to make his first thirty-

five-millimeter film, called *Amblin'*. It was about two young hitchhikers, a boy and a girl, who meet, spend a day together, and then part. Steven made it without dialogue, because it was cheaper that way. Even so, *Amblin'* was clever, funny, and original.

When film librarian Chuck Silvers saw *Amblin'*, he loved it. He called Sidney Sheinberg, an executive at Universal TV, and told him to drop everything—there was a film by a kid named Spielberg that he just had to see. After watching *Amblin'*, Sheinberg arranged to meet Steven the following day.

Sheinberg was surprised to see someone who looked like a teenager. But he could tell right away that Steven knew more about filmmaking than most pros twice his age. He also knew that Universal's busy television department needed directors. So he offered Steven a seven-year contract.

Steven confessed later, "I quit college so fast, I didn't even clean out my locker."

Chapter 4
TV Training Wheels

If Steven was nervous about directing an early episode of *Night Gallery*, a series of spooky half-hour shows with twisty surprise endings, he didn't show it. Even working with Joan Crawford, a movie star old enough to be his grandmother,

MOVIE TALK

PEOPLE IN THE FILM INDUSTRY USE LOTS OF INTERESTING WORDS AND EXPRESSIONS.

BLOCKBUSTER: A VERY, VERY SUCCESSFUL MOVIE

BOX OFFICE: THE TOTAL AMOUNT OF MONEY A FILM EARNS THROUGH TICKET SALES

CGI: COMPUTER-GENERATED IMAGES. FILM IMAGES AND SPECIAL EFFECTS CREATED ON A COMPUTER

FEATURE FILM: A MOVIE THAT IS AT LEAST FORTY MINUTES LONG. MOST FEATURE FILMS ARE AT LEAST AN HOUR LONG.

FRANCHISE: A MOVIE CAN BECOME A FRANCHISE IF IT BRANCHES OUT INTO SEQUELS, VIDEO GAMES, TELEVISION SHOWS, ACTION FIGURES, OR BOOKS.

GREEN LIGHT: GETTING A GREEN LIGHT MEANS THAT ENOUGH MONEY HAS BEEN RAISED FOR WORK ON A MOVIE TO START.

POSTPRODUCTION: THE PERIOD AFTER FILMING, OR PRINCIPAL PHOTOGRAPHY, IS COMPLETE. EDITING, ADDING THE SOUNDTRACK, AND PUTTING IN SPECIAL EFFECTS ARE ALL DONE IN POSTPRODUCTION.

SHORT FILM: A FILM THAT IS LESS THAN FORTY MINUTES LONG

SHOT 1.

ZOOM IN ON GRAVESTONE AT NIGHT

SHOT 2.

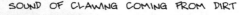

SOUND OF CLAWING COMING FROM DIRT

SHOT 3.

SILHOUETTE OF HAND BREAKING THROUGH

STORYBOARD: A SERIES OF DRAWINGS OR SKETCHES, LIKE A COMIC STRIP, SHOWING THE ACTION AND CAMERA ANGLES IN A MOVIE. THIS WAY OF PLANNING SCENES BEGAN IN THE 1930S, WITH WALT DISNEY AND HIS ANIMATORS. SOME DIRECTORS, LIKE STEVEN, STILL USE STORYBOARDS.

didn't seem to rattle him. He was all business on the set; he knew he had to be. A lot depended on this first job.

Steven charmed Joan Crawford, who could behave like Cruella De Vil if she chose, and she delivered a great performance for him. The finished show was as scary as it was supposed to be—and it aired on schedule. Executives at Universal were happy. In no time at all Steven had a real office at the studio, a new convertible, and a house of his own in Laurel Canyon. The one thing he didn't have was a green light, or go-ahead, to make a full-length feature film.

Steven directed many TV episodes and a handful of hour-long made-for-TV movies. One of them, called *Duel*, was an eerie, nearly wordless thriller that drew glowing reviews and was later released in European movie theaters. Critics praised *Duel* so highly that Steven got at least a dozen offers to direct feature films after its debut. But none of them intrigued him as much as a news story he had read about a young Texas couple called the Dents. They were so desperate to get their son back from a foster home that they became outlaws, and dozens of police cars chased them from one end of Texas to the other.

Steven knew the story would make a great movie. He also knew that it would require a budget of $2.5 million. He managed to get Universal to pay for him to write a script about the Dents, but that was all. Meanwhile, Richard Zanuck and David Brown, two talented producers, joined Universal and read the script. They decided they wanted to make the film, with Steven directing, and convinced the head of the studio to give Steven's movie idea a green light.

He began shooting *The Sugarland Express* in January 1973, a few weeks after his twenty-sixth birthday. Zanuck and Brown were amazed by how well "the kid" handled the shoot. He directed the actors, the fifty cars and drivers, and the many dangerous stunts like an old pro.

Though film critics loved *The Sugarland Express*, audiences didn't, and that was very disappointing to Steven. He knew that if his next movie wasn't a success, his career might be over.

Chapter 5
Shark Attack!

On a visit to the Brown/Zanuck offices one day in 1973, Steven noticed a copy of an unpublished novel on Zanuck's desk and read it over the weekend. Called *Jaws,* it was about a killer shark that terrorizes a small resort town. It hooked Steven right away, and the producers agreed to let him direct a film version. He was thrilled, but not for long. The shoot was plagued with problems from day one.

First, there was the location. Martha's Vineyard, a small island in Massachusetts, is a popular summer resort. In good weather its waters are crowded with yachts, sailboats, water-skiers, and swimmers. Steven couldn't show his shark hunters battling a great white with tourists on a fishing boat waving in the background. So almost every day, he and the crew had to wait for the ocean to clear. That took hours and hours of precious daylight, and the schedule slowed down to a crawl.

Then there was the weather. When it was stormy, sailors and tourists kept out of the water. But bad weather made shooting on the ocean difficult, dangerous, and sometimes impossible. That meant more delays.

And then there was the shark. The great white had to be so huge and scary that audiences would scream when it appeared. No real great white could be trained for a film, and it was decades before modern CGI, so a mechanical shark was made. Weighing twelve tons, it had cold, staring eyes; teeth as big as carving knives; and a body the size of a stretch limo. Steven named it Bruce, after his lawyer.

During the very first camera test, Bruce broke apart and sank straight to the ocean floor. He had to be towed away for three weeks' worth

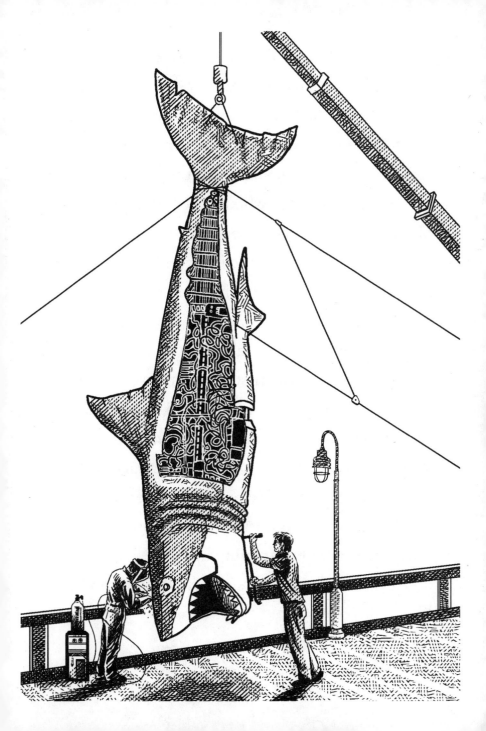

of repairs, a disaster for the film's schedule and budget. Because so much was going wrong, the crew started calling the movie *Flaws*. The actors wanted to quit. And there were rumblings at Universal about shutting down the movie.

Sidney Sheinberg, who by then was president of Universal, promised Steven his full support. Steven vowed to finish the film, and he did.

But even after it was edited and set to music, he worried that *Jaws* would flop. "I was out of my mind with fear," he said later. At an early screening, during the first gruesome shark attack, the man sitting next to him rushed out of the theater, gagging. *He'll never come back,* Steven thought miserably. But a few minutes later, the man did come back. He raced to his seat as if he couldn't stand to miss another second of the movie—even after throwing up.

At that moment, Steven knew *Jaws* would be a hit.

When it was released in the summer of 1975, critics were divided about *Jaws*, but not about Bruce: He was one *terrifying* shark. And suddenly everybody wanted to see him. So Universal tried something new. Instead of sending copies of the movie to a few theaters (which is what a studio usually did when a movie opened), Universal sent it to hundreds of theaters across the country, so everybody *could* see Bruce. The experiment worked: *Jaws* was a spectacular hit, the first-ever summer blockbuster. Earning a whopping $260 million, it also became the top-grossing film in history.

Already planning another film, Steven knew one thing for sure. "My next picture will be made on dry land," he said. "There won't even be a bathroom scene."

Chapter 6
Calling All Aliens

True to his word, Steven set his next picture far from the ocean (though it did have two bathroom scenes).

Much of *Close Encounters of the Third Kind* takes place in Wyoming, atop a mountain called Devils Tower. In science-fiction terms, an encounter of the first kind is a sighting of an

unidentified flying object (UFO). An encounter of the second kind is seeing or feeling the effects of the UFO. An encounter of the third kind is having direct contact with the UFO and its alien passengers.

The script, which Steven wrote, tells two stories. One is about Roy Neary, a man so obsessed with UFOs that he leaves his family to find them. The other is about Claude Lacombe, the leader of a top secret US project designed to make contact with aliens. The stories overlap when Roy and Claude meet at Devils Tower, just as a spectacular "close encounter of the third kind" with an enormous spaceship begins.

Steven based his screenplay on his own science-fiction movie *Firelight*, and on dozens of articles and books about UFOs. He read accounts of alien abductions, or kidnappings, and spoke with many scientists who thought there could be life in other parts of the universe.

When Steven wrote *Close Encounters of the Third Kind,* he decided that "there would be no bad guys in it." He made the alien visitors peaceful and very intelligent. Their spaceship is as big as a city. Its landing is dazzling, a special-effects extravaganza of light and sound. When the aliens invite Roy to leave Earth with them, he accepts happily.

SCIENCE FICTION IN THE MOVIES

SCIENCE FICTION ATTEMPTS TO DESCRIBE HOW PEOPLE MIGHT BE AFFECTED BY IMAGINARY SCIENTIFIC DEVELOPMENTS. SCIENCE-FICTION MOVIES ARE OFTEN ABOUT TIME TRAVEL, LIFE ON OTHER WORLDS, OR ARTIFICIAL INTELLIGENCE (COMPUTERS). MANY ARE SET IN THE FUTURE. SOME, LIKE *CLOSE ENCOUNTERS OF THE THIRD KIND* AND *E.T.: THE EXTRA-TERRESTRIAL*, TAKE PLACE IN THE PRESENT BUT INCLUDE ALIENS—CREATURES FROM OTHER PLANETS.

SOME OF THE BEST-KNOWN SCIENCE-FICTION MOVIES OF ALL TIME INCLUDE *2001: A SPACE ODYSSEY*, *PLANET OF THE APES*, *STAR WARS*, *ALIEN*, *BACK TO THE FUTURE*, *MEN IN BLACK*, *THE MATRIX*, *AVATAR*—AND, OF COURSE, *CLOSE ENCOUNTERS OF THE THIRD KIND*, *E.T.: THE EXTRA-TERRESTRIAL*, AND *JURASSIC PARK*.

Close Encounters of the Third Kind seems to be saying that life beyond our galaxy might be friendly. This hopeful message may be one reason why so many people—not all of them science-fiction fans—loved the movie. It made hundreds of millions of dollars and brought Steven his first Oscar nomination for Best Director.

Chapter 7
Indiana Jones and the Adventure That Just Wouldn't Stop

One day in 1977, two bearded men sat on a beach, deep in conversation. Anyone passing by would have thought they were ordinary tourists, enjoying yet another perfect day in Hawaii.

The truth was much more interesting.

The men were Steven Spielberg and the film director George Lucas, and they were talking about making a movie together. Friends since the late sixties, they had more in common than their age, their talent, and their beards. They both loved the Saturday-afternoon serials of their childhood. These short movies were shown in weekly segments, like chapters in a book, before

the main features. They were adventure stories, with wild chases and cliff-hanger endings. Their

heroes were daredevils—strong, brave, and reckless.

George told Steven that he'd been thinking about writing a serial-style movie script for a long time. The hero was a treasure-seeking archaeologist who cracked a mean bullwhip and wore a fedora hat. His name would be Indiana Smith. And the movie would be called *Raiders of the Lost Ark*.

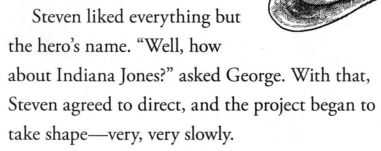

Steven liked everything but the hero's name. "Well, how about Indiana Jones?" asked George. With that, Steven agreed to direct, and the project began to take shape—very, very slowly.

Three years later (after Lucas's *Star Wars* had passed *Jaws* as the top-grossing film in history),

HARRISON FORD

George and Steven had a screenplay. They even had their Indiana Jones: Harrison Ford, who had played Han Solo in *Star Wars*.

While the new Indy began bullwhip lessons and the costume director tracked down the perfect 1930s-style fedora, Steven planned some of the movie's many action scenes on storyboards. Working on location in the North African country of Tunisia, he filmed quickly, with as few takes as possible. He had promised George, who was producing the film, that *Raiders of the Lost Ark* would stay on schedule.

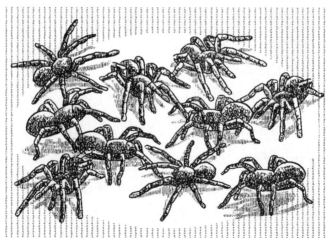

Despite blistering heat, a scene with 7,000 live snakes (including five deadly cobras), and another scene with hundreds of tarantulas, Steven finished almost two weeks early. The shoot had been fun, but exhausting.

When *Raiders* opened a few months later, it was a smash—the most successful film of 1981. Because of Indiana Jones, fedoras became popular again. There was a sudden demand for beat-up, Indy-style leather jackets.

And Steven Spielberg became a household name.

Chapter 8
A Friend from Far Away

Now that Steven was a celebrity, the public wanted to know everything about him, including what his childhood was like. When was he going to make a movie about *that*?

In many ways *E.T.: The Extra-Terrestrial* reflects feelings Steven had as a boy. Set in suburban California, it centers around the friendship between Elliott, a timid fifth-grader, and E.T., a toddler-size alien stranded on Earth. When E.T. is captured by government agents, Elliott finds the courage to plan a daring rescue. He gets E.T. back to his spaceship so that the little alien can return home.

Of course, Steven did not befriend an alien when he was a boy. But as an outsider in one

suburban town after another, he often imagined a friend like E.T. And the fantasy stayed with him. One night while he was on location for *Raiders of the Lost Ark*, Steven began writing a story about the little alien. "What if I were ten years old again," he wondered, "and he needed me as much as I needed him?"

Steven made *E.T.* almost entirely from Elliott's point of view. He shot the film so that audiences see what Elliott sees and understand how he feels. In Elliott's world, kids always keep secrets from grown-ups, hardly ever tell them the truth, and never doubt for a second that E.T. is worth fighting for. (Especially when E.T. makes their bikes fly.)

For audiences, Steven's skill with the young cast was just one of the film's many attractions. *E.T.* won praise for its script, its special effects, its photography, its music, and its editing. Steven was nominated for another Oscar, again for Best Director. As for E.T., the wrinkly, wobbly alien became America's weirdest little sweetheart. His plaintive cry, "E.T. phone home!" became the catchphrase of the year.

E.T. was Steven's biggest hit yet. It made more money than any other movie in history, topping *Jaws* and even *Star Wars*.

In 1984, Steven made his first sequel. *Indiana Jones and the Temple of Doom* was another action-packed, sometimes-gruesome movie adventure, this time set in India. The heroine, a blond nightclub singer, was played by actress Kate Capshaw. In the movie, a hungry elephant eats her best costume. Boa constrictors hug her. She's

served eyeball soup and monkey brains for dinner. And she breaks at least two fingernails—all before Indy even kisses her.

The tremendous success of *E.T.* and *Temple of Doom* gave Steven a lot more creative freedom. He would still direct the kind of action adventures and summer blockbusters that audiences wanted from him. They were his "popcorn movies." They had made him famous, but now he could make more serious films, too.

Chapter 9
Turning Points

Steven called his next film "my first serious movie." *The Color Purple*, based on the book by Alice Walker, is about two African American sisters in rural Georgia who are cruelly separated in their early teens. It's set mainly in the 1930s, and almost all the characters are African American.

Many of them are women whose struggles are harsh and disturbing. And there isn't a single explosion or alien in the entire story.

Making *The Color Purple* marked a turning point in Steven's career. There was another important turning point in Steven's life that year: He and his longtime girlfriend, actress Amy Irving, had a son together. They named him Max and married soon after the baby was born.

Though being a new father took a lot of Steven's time, he still worked twice as hard as most other people in Hollywood. He wrote successful screenplays for other directors, produced films, and embarked on his first big historical epic.

Empire of the Sun is about the Japanese invasion of China during World War II. The movie has thousands and thousands of extras and dozens of speaking parts. There are huge, powerful crowd scenes. But the story hits home

because Steven tells it from a young boy's point of view. Jamie, the son of wealthy English parents, must fend for himself after the invasion. Jamie is played by Christian Bale, and, like some other child actors who worked with Steven, he went on to become very famous.

Steven loved being a father and yearned for a close, loving family—something he hadn't always had when he was growing up. But in 1989 his marriage to Amy Irving ended. They agreed to raise Max jointly.

Steven said very little about his divorce.
Instead, he worked harder than ever. He made a
romantic ghost story called *Always*, and a third
Indiana Jones movie, *Indiana Jones and the Last
Crusade*. He produced an Indiana Jones television

special and the film *Back to the Future Part II*.

Meanwhile, Kate Capshaw, the actress from *Temple of Doom*, reentered his life. Steven had once said that the best thing about making that movie "was that I met Kate Capshaw." They fell in love, and after she converted to Judaism, they married.

KATE CAPSHAW

As newlyweds, Steven and Kate already had a fair-size family. There was Max, Steven's son, and Jessica, Kate's daughter with her first husband. There was Theo, Kate's adopted African American son. And there was Sasha, the daughter Steven and Kate had together in 1990.

With a fresh crop of grandchildren to love, Steven's mother, Leah, drew closer to her son again. The only person missing from this new family picture was Steven's father, Arnold. He and Steven hadn't spoken to each other in many years, because Steven had never forgiven Arnold for his parents' divorce. Kate felt this had to change. She

persuaded Steven to contact his father, and once
he did, the long silence between them ended.
Now that he was a father himself, Steven could
understand Arnold better. And the two, once
again, became very close.

Chapter 10
Raptors and Oscars

Steven had always wanted to make a dinosaur movie. When he read Michael Crichton's 1990 novel *Jurassic Park*, he knew it was the story he'd been looking for. Scientists find insects that had fed on dinosaur blood trapped in amber, preserving the dinosaurs' DNA. John Hammond, who is rich enough to own a large tropical island, gets hold of the DNA and uses it to clone dinosaurs. Before long, herds of them are roaming a huge enclosure on Hammond's island.

Jurassic Park, as Hammond calls it, will soon
be the greatest tourist attraction of all time.
Before it opens, three scientists and Hammond's
grandchildren come for a preview.

Then the dinosaurs get loose. The scariest is
the angry *Tyrannosaurus rex*, who makes the
shark in *Jaws* look like a bath toy. Making *Jurassic*

Park almost twenty years after *Jaws*, Steven could use the newest, most advanced CGI effects. They were amazing. "This was the first movie ever made," he said, "where the entire success or failure of the story was dependent on these digital characters." The film was a landmark in visual effects and earned an unprecedented $914 million worldwide.

Steven did postproduction work on *Jurassic Park* at night in Poland, and filmed *Schindler's List* during the day.

Based on a true story, it's about a German businessman, Oskar Schindler, who comes to Nazi-occupied Poland during World War II, hoping to profit from the war.

OSKAR SCHINDLER

THE NAZI PARTY

THE NAZI PARTY WAS A GERMAN POLITICAL GROUP THAT BEGAN IN 1919. THE NAZIS BELIEVED THAT "ARYANS"—WHITE PROTESTANT GERMANS— WERE BETTER THAN PEOPLE OF ANY OTHER RACE.

ADOLF HITLER BECAME THE DICTATOR (OR FüHRER) OF NAZI GERMANY IN 1934. HIS GOVERNMENT STARTED TO KILL OFF ALL "IMPURE" PEOPLE UNDER GERMAN RULE, INCLUDING JEWS, ROMANIES, HOMOSEXUALS, CATHOLICS, AND THE MENTALLY CHALLENGED. THE NAZIS' CAREFULLY PLANNED PROGRAM OF MASS MURDER TOOK A TOTAL OF ELEVEN MILLION LIVES; SIX MILLION VICTIMS WERE JEWS. THESE MURDERS ARE KNOWN AS THE HOLOCAUST.

NAZI RULE ENDED IN 1945, WITH GERMANY'S DEFEAT IN WORLD WAR II.

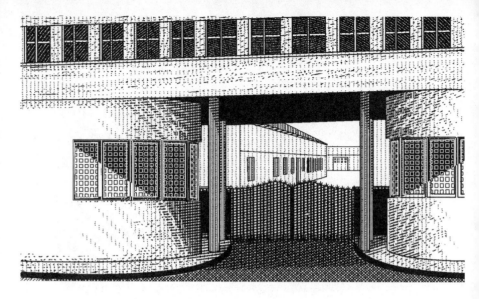

    While Nazis are taking away Jews' property
and making it illegal for them to earn money,
Schindler sets up a factory in the city of Kraków.
He hires only Jewish workers and quickly makes
a fortune.

    Schindler does not come to Poland to save
Jews. He is not a very noble man—at first. But
when he sees what is happening around him, he
changes. Using charm, cunning, and huge bribes,
he persuades the Nazis to leave his workers alone.
He risks his life more than once and loses most

of his money. His bravery and generosity save the lives of 1,100 people.

Making *Schindler's List* was intensely painful for Steven. During the Holocaust, the Nazis had killed many relatives on his father's side of the family who had lived in Russia and Poland. Steven wanted the film to honor them, and to honor the millions of other victims who died. He also wanted his children to understand this terrible time in Jewish history. "It was the first time my children ever saw me cry," he said.

When *Schindler's List* opened, audiences cried, too. Though it was sad and sometimes shocking, it also showed courage and decency overcoming terrible evil. The film won the Oscar for Best Feature Film of 1993, and Steven won his first Oscar for Best Director.

WHO IS OSCAR?

OSCAR, THE GOLD-PLATED STATUETTE GIVEN OUT AT THE ACADEMY AWARDS CEREMONY EVERY YEAR, IS PROBABLY THE MOST FAMOUS TROPHY IN THE WORLD. IT IS ALSO CONSIDERED THE HIGHEST POSSIBLE HONOR IN FILMMAKING. EACH OSCAR IS AWARDED AFTER A SECRET VOTE BY THE ACADEMY OF

MOTION PICTURE ARTS AND SCIENCES, WHICH HAS THOUSANDS OF MEMBERS. THOUGH ITS OFFICIAL NAME IS THE ACADEMY AWARD OF MERIT, THE AWARD IS ALMOST ALWAYS CALLED "THE OSCAR." NOBODY KNOWS EXACTLY WHY. ONE POPULAR STORY IS THAT ON FIRST SEEING THE STATUETTE, THE ACADEMY LIBRARIAN SAID IT LOOKED JUST LIKE HER UNCLE OSCAR.

THE FIRST ACADEMY AWARDS WERE PRESENTED IN 1929, AT A SMALL HOTEL DINNER. SINCE THEN, THOUSANDS OF ACADEMY AWARDS HAVE BEEN GIVEN OUT. AN OSCAR NOMINATION HAS BECOME A HIGH HONOR IN ITSELF. A WIN PRACTICALLY GUARANTEES FAME AND MONEY. BECAUSE THE

NAMES OF WINNERS ARE KEPT SECRET, THE
SUSPENSE, BOTH BEFORE AND DURING THE
CEREMONY, RUNS HIGH. EXPERIENCED PERFORMERS
OFTEN BREAK INTO TEARS WHEN THEIR NAMES ARE
CALLED.

THE ACADEMY AWARDS CEREMONY IS NOW
TELEVISED IN MORE THAN 200 COUNTRIES. FOR
HUNDREDS OF MILLIONS OF MOVIE FANS ALL OVER
THE WORLD, SHARING THE EXCITEMENT IS A HIGH
POINT OF EACH YEAR.

Chapter 11
Dream Company

After the 1994 Academy Awards, Steven took a break from moviemaking to spend time with his family. By now he had five children: Max, Jessica, Theo, Sasha, and Sawyer, a son born in 1992.

During this time, Steven's friends Jeffrey Katzenberg and David Geffen approached him about starting a film studio together. It was a daring idea; nobody had launched a new studio for decades because it was so difficult and expensive. Yet Jeffrey Katzenberg had produced a string of animated megahits for Disney, including *The Little Mermaid*, *Beauty and the Beast*, and *The Lion King*. David Geffen, whose work in the music business had made him a billionaire, was one of entertainment's most powerful deal makers. Steven was now considered the world's most successful director. If anybody could launch a new studio, it was these three.

Steven decided to join Jeffrey and David on three conditions. First, they wouldn't make more than nine movies a year; second, he would be free to direct for other studios; and third, he would leave work every day in time to have dinner with his family. They agreed, and in October 1994, DreamWorks Studios opened for business.

Steven's first film for DreamWorks was *Amistad*, based on the true story of a slave-ship mutiny in 1839.

Captured by traders, chained and beaten, the Africans on the *Amistad* know that slavery awaits them when they reach Cuba. So they take over

the ship and sail north. Then they are caught off
the coast of Long Island and accused of murder.
With the help of antislavery groups and former
president John Quincy Adams, the Africans win

their freedom, though it takes many years. There is a powerful message about the need for tolerance and human kindness in *Amistad*, just as there is in *Schindler's List* and *E.T.*

Steven said that he made *Amistad* for his adopted African American son, Theo. His next DreamWorks film was for his father, whose stories about serving in World War II had

fascinated him when he was a boy.

An early scene in *Saving Private Ryan* begins on June 6, 1944, when American troops lead a massive surprise attack (called D-day) against the Germans on France's northern coast. The long scene, which looks as real as a documentary, shows hundreds of soldiers dying under heavy German fire.

Saving Private Ryan was a tribute to all the American soldiers who risked their lives in World War II.

Steven knew that, like *Schindler's List*, the movie could be painful to watch, and he was prepared for audiences to stay away. But they didn't. *Saving Private Ryan* was the most successful American film of 1998. It was nominated for eleven Academy Awards and won Steven his second Oscar for Best Director.

Chapter 12
Long-Term Projects

Steven turned fifty-five years old in 2001. He had won three Academy Awards. He ran a movie business with two good friends. He was closer to his parents than ever before, and his own family life was happy. He was a man who had everything—except a college degree. So that year he reenrolled at California State University, Long Beach, took courses in their new film department, and graduated on May 31, 2002—nearly forty years after he had dropped out.

The theme from *Indiana Jones and the Raiders of the Lost Ark* played as he accepted his diploma.

Steven kept making feature films; he directed six between 2001 and 2005. For anyone else, that would have been a lot. For Steven, who was also producing movies and television shows, creating video games, writing, supporting charities, and being a family man, it was life as usual. He liked to keep busy.

Fans had been asking for another Indiana Jones adventure since the third one, *Indiana Jones and the Last Crusade* in 1989. Nineteen years later, Steven finally made it for them.

Indiana Jones and the Kingdom of the Crystal Skull takes place in the 1950s, when Indy is a lot older. But he's still tough enough to stop an evil Russian agent from brainwashing him.

Fans loved the older Indy, still played by Harrison Ford. They welcomed his teenage-rebel sidekick, who turns out to be his son. And they were glad to see him marry Marion Ravenwood, the girlfriend who punched him in the jaw in *Raiders of the Lost Ark*. Indy number four earned $800 million at the box office.

Back in 1981, when *Raiders* first came out, Steven had read a review of the film that compared Indiana Jones to Tintin. Steven found out that Tintin was a Belgian comic-strip character, and that practically every kid in Europe was a huge fan. He decided Tintin's exciting adventures, like Indy's, would make a great movie. He bought the rights but got stuck deciding if the movie should be animated or not.

Years went by. In 2006, director Peter Jackson persuaded Steven to make the movie in 3-D using performance capture. This technology can take an actor's live performance on film and turn it into a completely lifelike computer-generated character. Steven had admired Peter's use of performance capture in the *Lord of the Rings* movies. The two men were also friends, so it seemed natural for them to work together on *The Adventures of Tintin*, with Steven directing and Peter producing.

Although Steven finished filming the actors in 2009, the computer artists would need at least two years to complete the film. During that time, he made another movie.

War Horse is about an English boy called Albert and his beloved horse, Joey. When World War I begins, Joey is sold to an English captain and taken to fight in France.

As the war drags on, Joey moves from one owner to the next. He experiences battles that are almost as frightening as the ones in *Saving Private Ryan*. Eventually, Albert finds him and saves his life, just as the war ends. *War Horse* is an epic story, once again stressing the importance of loyalty, trust, and friendship.

Steven had spent almost thirty years preparing for *The Adventures of Tintin*, and less than a year on *War Horse*. Yet *War Horse* earned six Academy Award nominations. Also released in 2011, *Tintin* earned over $300 million worldwide.

Chapter 13
History Master

Steven had been thinking about making *Lincoln* for a very long time. He was finally able to start working on it in 2011, a year that marked the 150th anniversary of the start of the American Civil War.

Lincoln takes place in 1865, during the last months of the president's life. The Civil War is coming to a close after four bloody years. Lincoln knows the North will win, and he wants to end slavery once and for all.

In the film, Lincoln faces three obstacles. He must unite the quarrelsome advisers in his cabinet so they stand behind him. He must win support for an amendment to the Constitution that will abolish slavery. And he must delay peace talks with the South until the amendment is passed.

In *Lincoln*, we see the president not just as the great leader depicted in history books but as a shrewd politician who does whatever needs to be done to get the amendment passed. Scene by scene, the film shows us Lincoln's charm and powerful will. Long before the movie is over, we understand exactly why he deserves his place in history. A powerful reflection of Steven's lifelong interest in Abraham Lincoln, it opened to glowing reviews in late 2012.

Steven Spielberg has never settled for being just a super successful Hollywood director. He has always made the movies he wanted to make. He has also encouraged and supported young filmmakers. He has founded charities and museums. He has been honored by the US Army,

the US Navy, and the White House. He was made a knight of the British Empire by Queen Elizabeth II, given a Knight Commander's Cross of the Order of Merit by the government of Germany, and made a Commander of the Order of the Crown in Belgium.

His films have set and broken box-office records for decades. They often show how acts of personal courage can change history. They have made people—millions and millions of people— laugh, cry, cheer, and hyperventilate.

And it all started in 1957, when he borrowed his father's movie camera.

TIMELINE OF
STEVEN SPIELBERG'S LIFE

1946	Born December 18 in Cincinnati, Ohio
1952	Sees his first movie, Cecil B. DeMille's *The Greatest Show on Earth*
1957	Uses his father's Brownie camera to make *The Last Train Wreck* (three minutes)
1964	Moves to California with his family
1967	Meets George Lucas
1969	Signs seven-year contract with Universal Studios Television; drops out of college
1975	Becomes a millionaire
1984	Forms production company Amblin Entertainment with Kathleen Kennedy, and produces *Gremlins*, directed by Joe Dante
1985	Marries Amy Irving
1987	Wins Irving G. Thalberg Memorial Award for excellence in movie production
1989	Divorces Amy Irving
1991	Marries Kate Capshaw
1992	Uses CGI for the first time in *Jurassic Park*
1994	Establishes Survivors of the Shoah Visual History Foundation to videotape Holocaust survivors
1999	Named Best Director of the 20th Century by *Entertainment Weekly*
2001	Produces *Shrek* and *Band of Brothers*
2002	Graduates from California State University, Long Beach, with a BA in film
2011	Works with Peter Jackson on *The Adventures of Tintin*

TIMELINE OF
THE WORLD

Slavery abolished in the United States	1865
First UFO sighted in the United States	1898
Charlie Chaplin, Mary Pickford, D. W. Griffith, and Douglas Fairbanks form United Artists Studio	1919
Walt Disney creates Mickey Mouse	1928
First Academy Awards are held	1929
Nazis invade Poland; World War II begins	1939
The United States enters World War II	1941
Legal segregation in American public schools ends	1954
The Beatles come to America	1964
CGI used for the first time in a feature film	1967
Vietnam War ends	1975
First personal computers are sold	1977
First Sundance Film Festival is held	1978
Terrorists attack the World Trade Center and the Pentagon	2001
Barack Obama is elected president	2008
Kathryn Bigelow is first woman to win an Oscar for Best Director	2010

BIBLIOGRAPHY

Baxter, John. **Steven Spielberg: The Unauthorized Biography**. New York: Harper & Row, 1996.

Bernstein, Fred A. "Steven Spielberg's mother." In **The Jewish Mothers' Hall of Fame**, Doubleday, 1986.

Bill, Tony. **Movie Speak: How to Talk Like You Belong on a Film Set**. New York: Workman Publishing, 2008.

Corliss, Richard, and Jeffrey Ressner. "Peter Pan Grows Up But Can He Still Fly?" **TIME Magazine**, May 19, 1997.

Ebert, Roger, and Gene Siskel. **The Future of the Movies: Interviews with Martin Scorsese, Steven Spielberg, and George Lucas**. Kansas City, MO: Andrews and McMeel, 1991.

Friedman, Lester D., and Brent Notbohm, eds. **Steven Spielberg: Interviews**. Jackson: University Press of Mississippi, 2000.

McBride, Joseph. **Steven Spielberg: A Biography**, 2nd ed. Jackson: University Press of Mississippi, 2010.

Rubin, Susan Goldman. **Steven Spielberg: Crazy for Movies**. New York: Harry N. Abrams, 2001.

Schickel, Richard. **Steven Spielberg: A Retrospective**. New York: Sterling, 2012.

Spielberg, Steven. Interview, **Close Encounters of the Third Kind**, collector's ed. DVD, 1998.

Spielberg, Steven. Interview with James Lipton. **Live at the Actor's Studio**, February 14, 1999.

Spielberg, Steven. **Schindler's List: Director's Statement**. DVD, 1993.

"Steven Spielberg To Graduate from California State University, Long Beach With Bachelor's Degree in Film and Electronic Arts." **CSU Newsline**, May 14, 2002. http://www.calstate.edu/newsline/Archive/01-02/020514-LB.shtml.

Tugend, Tom. "A close encounter with Steven Spielberg's dad," **Jewish Journal**, June 13, 2012, http://www.jewishjournal.com/hollywood/article/a_close_encounter_with_steven_spielbergs_dad_20120613.

FILMOGRAPHY

1964 *Firelight*

1972 *Duel* (expanded from TV version)

1974 *The Sugarland Express*

1975 *Jaws*

1977 *Close Encounters of the Third Kind*

1979 *1941*

1981 *Raiders of the Lost Ark* (later retitled *Indiana Jones and the Raiders of the Lost Ark*)

1982 *E.T.: The Extra-Terrestrial*

1983 *Twilight Zone: The Movie* (directed one 23-minute "episode")

1984 *Indiana Jones and the Temple of Doom*

1985 *The Color Purple*

1987 *Empire of the Sun*

1989 *Indiana Jones and the Last Crusade*; *Always*

1991 *Hook*

1993 *Jurassic Park*; *Schindler's List*

1997 *The Lost World: Jurassic Park*; *Amistad*

1998 *Saving Private Ryan*

2001 *A.I.: Artificial Intelligence*

2002 *Minority Report*; *Catch Me If You Can*

2004 *The Terminal*

2005 *War of the Worlds*; *Munich*

2008 *Indiana Jones and the Kingdom of the Crystal Skull*

2011 *War Horse*; *The Adventures of Tintin*

2012 *Lincoln*